HAL•LEONARD UKULELE PLAY-ALONG

VOL. 11

Christmas STRUMMING

T0033885

Ukulele by Curt Mychael

Tracking, mixing, and mastering by
Jake Johnson and Chris Kringel

To access audio visit:
www.halleonard.com/mylibrary

4989-9262-2580-9217

ISBN 978-1-4584-1003-02

HAL•LEONARD®

Visit Hal Leonard Online at
www.halleonard.com

Contact us:
Hal Leonard
7777 West Bluemound Road
Milwaukee, WI 53213
Email: info@halleonard.com

In Europe, contact:
Hal Leonard Europe Limited
42 Wigmore Street
Marylebone, London, W1U 2RN
Email: info@halleonardeurope.com

In Australia, contact:
Hal Leonard Australia Pty. Ltd.
4 Lentara Court
Cheltenham, Victoria, 3192 Australia
Email: info@halleonard.com.au

Away in a Manger

Words by John T. McFarland (v. 3)
Music by James R. Murray

Deck the Hall

Traditional Welsh Carol

The First Noël

17th Century English Carol
Music from W. Sandys' Christmas Carols

Additional Lyrics

4. The star drew nigh to the northwest,
   O'er Bethlehem it took its rest;
   And there it did both stop and stay,
   Right over the place where Jesus lay.

5. Then entered in those wise men three,
   Full reverently upon their knee;
   And offered there in His presence,
   Their gold, and myrrh, and frankincense.

Hark! The Herald Angels Sing

Words by Charles Wesley
Altered by George Whitefield
Music by Felix Mendelssohn-Bartholdy

G
C
D7
Joy - ful all ye na - tions rise.
Veil'd in flesh the God - head see.
Mild, He lays His glo - ry by.
G
C
D7
Join the tri - umph of the skies.
Hail th' In - car - nate De - i - ty.
Born that man no more may die.
C
E7
Am
E7
Am
D7
G
With th'an - gel - ic host pro - claim, "Christ is born in
Pleased as man with man to dwell, Je - sus our Em -
Born to raise the sons of earth, born to give them
D7
G
C
E7
Am
E7
Am
Beth - le - hem."
man - u - el!
sec - ond birth.
Hark! The her - ald an - gels sing,
1., 2.
3.
D7
G
D7
G
D7
G
rit.
"Glo - ry to the new - born King!" new - born King!"

Jingle Bells

Words and Music by J. Pierpont

Chorus
G
D
G
night!
shot!
lead!
Oh!
Jin - gle bells,
jin - gle bells,
jin - gle all the way.
C
Oh, what fun it
G
A7
D
is to ride in a one horse o - pen sleigh!
G
Jin - gle bells, jin - gle bells, jin - gle all the
C
G
way. Oh, what fun it is to ride in a
1., 2.
3.
D
G
G
one horse o - pen sleigh! 2. A sleigh!

Joy to the World

Words by Isaac Watts
Music by George Frideric Handel
Adapted by Lowell Mason

heav - en and na - ture ___ sing, and ___
won - ders of His ___ love, and ___

A7
heav - en and na - ture ___ sing, and ___
won - ders of His ___ love, and ___

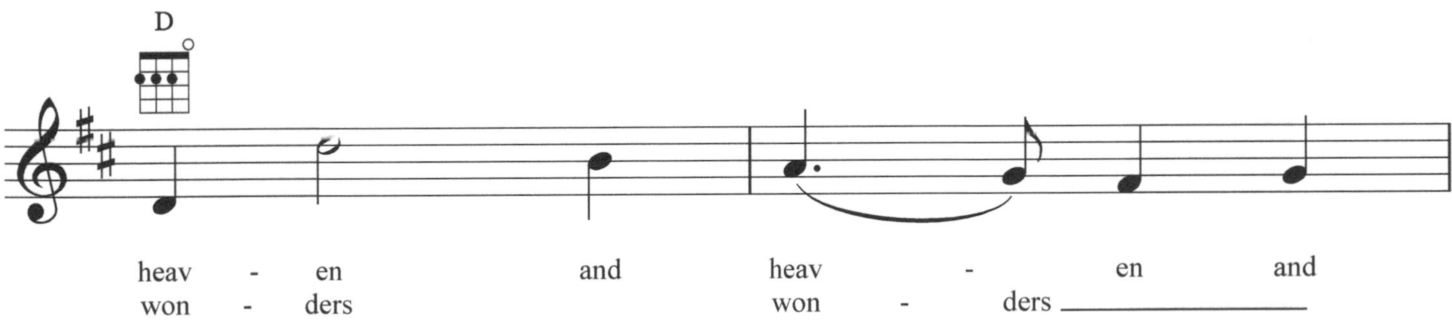
D
heav - en and heav - en and
won - ders won - ders ___

A7
1.
D
2.
D
na - ture sing. love.
of His

O Come, All Ye Faithful

(Adeste Fideles)

Music by John Francis Wade
Latin Words translated by Frederick Oakeley

Chorus
D
G
D
an - gels;
high - est.
O come, let us a -

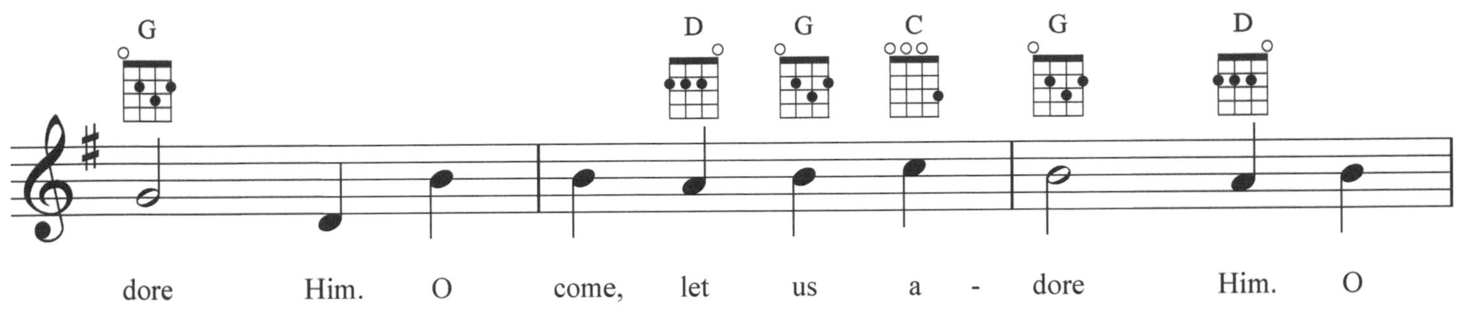
G
D
G
C
G
D
dore Him. O come, let us a - dore Him. O

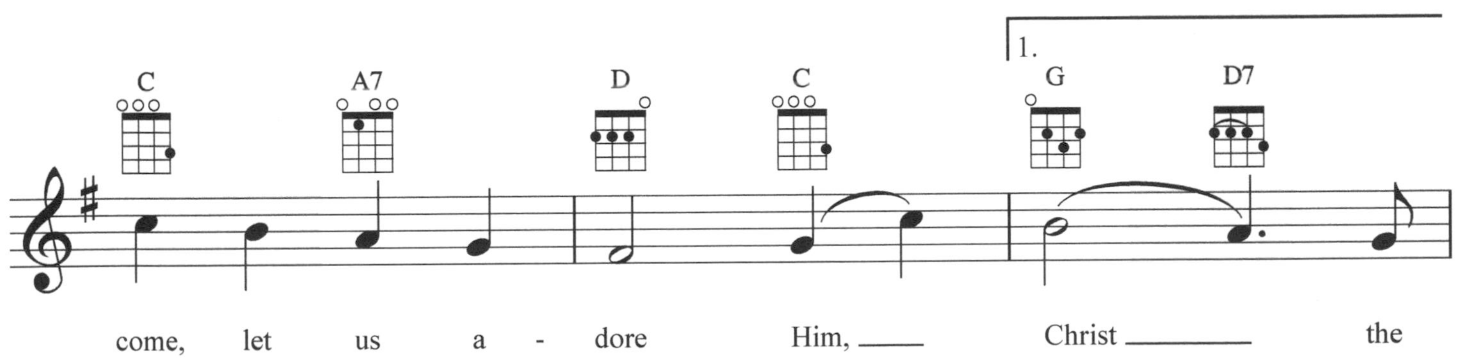
C
A7
D
C
1.
G
D7
come, let us a - dore Him, Christ the

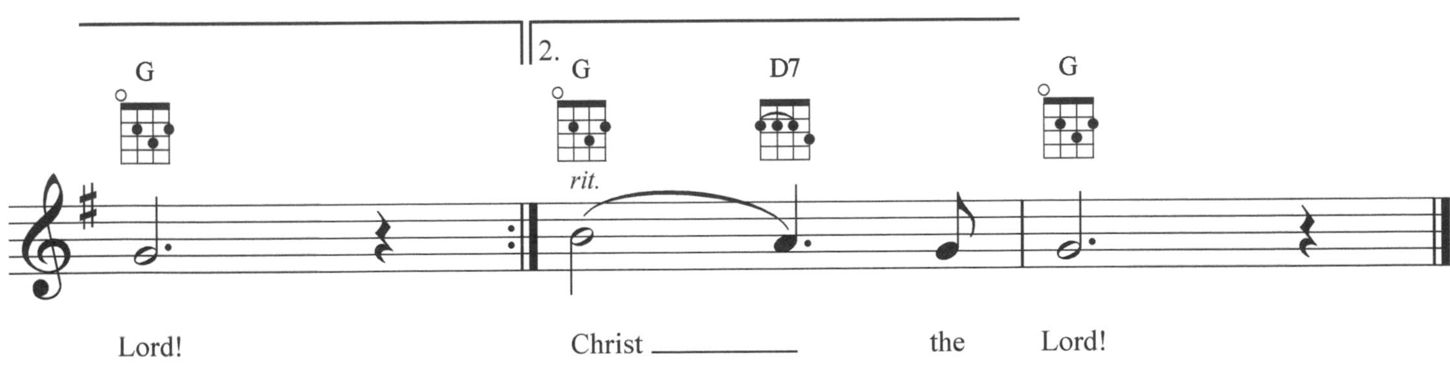
G
2.
G
D7
G
rit.
Lord! Christ the Lord!

We Three Kings of Orient Are

Words and Music by John H. Hopkins, Jr.

Chorus
D7
G
O, ___ star of won - der,
C
G
star of night, star with
C
G
roy - al beau - ty bright.
Em
D
C
D
West - ward lead - ing, still pro - ceed - ing,
G
C
G
guide us to thy per - fect light.

HAL•LEONARD®

UKULELE PLAY-ALONG

Now you can play your favorite songs on your uke with great-sounding backing tracks to help you sound like a bona fide pro! The audio also features playback tools so you can adjust the tempo without changing the pitch and loop challenging parts.

AUDIO ACCESS INCLUDED

1. POP HITS
00701451 Book/CD Pack $15.99

2. UKE CLASSICS
00701452 Book/CD Pack $15.99

3. HAWAIIAN FAVORITES
00701453 Book/Online Audio $14.99

4. CHILDREN'S SONGS
00701454 Book/Online Audio $14.99

5. CHRISTMAS SONGS
00701696 Book/CD Pack $12.99

6. LENNON & MCCARTNEY
00701723 Book/Online Audio $12.99

7. DISNEY FAVORITES
00701724 Book/Online Audio $12.99

8. CHART HITS
00701745 Book/CD Pack $15.99

9. THE SOUND OF MUSIC
00701784 Book/CD Pack $14.99

10. MOTOWN
00701964 Book/CD Pack $12.99

11. CHRISTMAS STRUMMING
00702458 Book/Online Audio $12.99

12. BLUEGRASS FAVORITES
00702584 Book/CD Pack $12.99

13. UKULELE SONGS
00702599 Book/CD Pack $12.99

14. JOHNNY CASH
00702615 Book/CD Pack $15.99

15. COUNTRY CLASSICS
00702834 Book/CD Pack $12.99

16. STANDARDS
00702835 Book/CD Pack $12.99

17. POP STANDARDS
00702836 Book/CD Pack $12.99

18. IRISH SONGS
00703086 Book/Online Audio $12.99

19. BLUES STANDARDS
00703087 Book/CD Pack $12.99

20. FOLK POP ROCK
00703088 Book/CD Pack $12.99

21. HAWAIIAN CLASSICS
00703097 Book/CD Pack $12.99

22. ISLAND SONGS
00703098 Book/CD Pack $12.99

23. TAYLOR SWIFT – 2ND EDITION
00221966 Book/Online Audio $16.99

24. WINTER WONDERLAND
00101871 Book/CD Pack $12.99

25. GREEN DAY
00110398 Book/CD Pack $14.99

26. BOB MARLEY
00110399 Book/Online Audio $14.99

27. TIN PAN ALLEY
00116358 Book/CD Pack $12.99

28. STEVIE WONDER
00116736 Book/CD Pack $14.99

29. OVER THE RAINBOW & OTHER FAVORITES
00117076 Book/Online Audio $14.99

30. ACOUSTIC SONGS
00122336 Book/CD Pack $14.99

31. JASON MRAZ
00124166 Book/CD Pack $14.99

32. TOP DOWNLOADS
00127507 Book/CD Pack $14.99

33. CLASSICAL THEMES
00127892 Book/Online Audio $14.99

34. CHRISTMAS HITS
00128602 Book/CD Pack $14.99

35. SONGS FOR BEGINNERS
00129009 Book/Online Audio $14.99

36. ELVIS PRESLEY HAWAII
00138199 Book/Online Audio $14.99

37. LATIN
00141191 Book/Online Audio $14.99

38. JAZZ
00141192 Book/Online Audio $14.99

39. GYPSY JAZZ
00146559 Book/Online Audio $14.99

40. TODAY'S HITS
00160845 Book/Online Audio $14.99

Prices, contents, and availability subject to change without notice.

www.halleonard.com

0719
483